Sisters

Sisters

Raina Telgemeier

with color by Braden Lamb

graphix

An Imprint of
SCHOLASTIC

For Amara, obviously

Library of Congress Cataloging-in-Publication Data

Telgemeier, Raina.
Sisters / Raina Telgemeier.
p. cm
Audience: Grade 4 to 6
ISBN 978-0-545-54059-9 (hardcover)
ISBN 978-0-545-54060-5 (paperback)
1. Brothers and sisters–Juvenile literature. 2. Families–Juvenile literature.
3. Interpersonal relations–Juvenile literature. I. Title.
HQ759.96.T46 2014
306.875'3–dc23
2013008700

10 9 8 7 6 5 4 3   14 15 16 17 18

First edition, September 2014
Edited by Cassandra Pelham
Lettering by John Green
Book design by Phil Falco
Creative Director: David Saylor
Printed in the U.S.A.   88

ARE YOU SURE YOU'RE ALL PACKED? YOU'RE NOT FORGETTING ANYTHING?

WHAT ABOUT THE TENT?

YES, I PACKED THE TENT.

WHAT ABOUT FLARES? BATTERIES? EXTRA WATER?

DENIS, WE'RE ONLY DRIVING FROM CALIFORNIA TO COLORADO!

YEAH, WHY ARE **YOU** SO STRESSED?

YOU'RE NOT EVEN COMING!

MAPS! DO YOU HAVE THE MAPS?

DADDY, WHY AREN'T YOU DRIVING TO AUNT MARY'S WITH US?

I'VE TOLD YOU, WILL . . .

I HAVE WORK THIS WEEK. MAKES MORE SENSE FOR ME TO TAKE A PLANE AND MEET YOU GUYS THERE.

OH.

ARE YOU EXCITED ABOUT SEEING YOUR COUSINS, RAINA?

I DUNNO.

WE HAVEN'T HAD A FAMILY REUNION IN ALMOST TEN YEARS!

I THOUGHT THAT WAS 'CAUSE YOU DIDN'T GET ALONG WITH YOUR SIBLINGS.

SPEAKING OF WHICH . . .

AMARA! RAINA!

HOW DO YOU EXPECT TO SURVIVE A WEEK IN THE CAR TOGETHER IF YOU CAN'T EVEN GET THROUGH **DINNER?**

I REALLY WISH YOU'D TAKE MY CAR INSTEAD. IT'S NEWER.

YOUR CAR IS TOO SMALL. MINE IS FINE.

I BET **YOU** WISH WE WERE TAKING DAD'S CAR, TOO...

ESPECIALLY CONSIDERING... "THE INCIDENT."

HAAA-HAAAH.

WHY DID I EVER ASK FOR A SISTER?!

SPLASH

6

RAINA . . . I'M GOING TO BE HAVING A BABY.

A GIRL?!

WELL . . . WE WON'T KNOW UNTIL IT GETS HERE.

IT BETTER BE A GIRL.

EITHER WAY, YOU'RE GOING TO BE A GOOD BIG SISTER!

YOU CAN HELP FEED THE BABY AND HOLD IT AND CARE FOR IT . . .

BUT SOON

HEY, MOM?

WHAT'S ALL THIS STUFF DOING IN MY ROOM?

7

A FEW MONTHS LATER

IT'S A CARD FOR WHEN MOM BRINGS THE BABY HOME FROM THE HOSPITAL, GRANDMA!

VERY NICE!

RING!

SHE DID? IT IS? I'LL PUT RAINA ON!

RAINA? IT'S DADDY! YOU HAVE A NEW BABY SISTER!

EEEEEEEEEEEEEE!!!!!

WE'RE HEEERE!

RAINA, MEET YOUR **SISTER!**

YOU'RE SURE THIS IS A GIRL?

UH-HUH . . .

PROVE IT.

GIRLS, HAVE YOU FINISHED PACKING?

WE LEAVE FIRST THING IN THE MORNING! **GO!**

WHAT DO PEOPLE EVEN WEAR IN COLORADO?

WILL MY COUSINS THINK MY CLOTHES ARE COOL?

Ooo

Knock

Knock

Aptos Tigers

YES?

ARE YOU HAVING A FASHION SHOW IN HERE OR SOMETHING?

WHAT? NO! DON'T COME IN!

I STILL DON'T SEE WHY MOM AND DAD GAVE **YOU** YOUR OWN ROOM.

BECAUSE I'M STARTING HIGH SCHOOL NEXT MONTH, AND I NEED MY PRIVACY.

THAT'S DUMB. ANYWAY, DO YOU HAVE ANY COLORED PENCILS?

WHAT FOR?

THE TRIP. WE'RE GONNA BE IN THE CAR FOR A WHOLE WEEK IN BOTH DIRECTIONS.

NOPE, NO COLORED PENCILS **HERE**. NOW GET OUT.

14

18

YOU CAN SIT WHEREVER YOU WANT TO. I DON'T CARE.

WHATEVER MAKES YOU HAPPY.

sniff

♪ ♫ ♫ ♪

crunch
crunch

IT'S GETTING HOT, MOM.

I KNOW. I'M SORRY MY CAR DOESN'T HAVE AIR-CONDITIONING.

BUT I CAN OPEN A WINDOW!

WHOOSH

squeaky squeaky

〜〜〜〜〜〜!

WHAT???

34

. . . IN A DEEP, WOODED THICKET . . .

RAINA

HI, GIRLS. WHAT ARE YOU DRAWING TODAY?

I'M DRAWING A FLOWER AND A SUN!

NICE, RAINA.

I DAWING A GIZZLY BEAR BY A STREAM, AN' A DEER, AN' A EAGLE, AN' ANOTHER DEER . . . AND OVER HERE . . .

TODAY WE DRIVE ACROSS NEVADA!

THE SILVER STATE.

LOOKS MORE LIKE THE BROWN STATE.

OR THE BURNT SIENNA STATE.

CLOSER TO RAW UMBER.

OR MAYBE BEIGE.

KHAKI?

SO . . . ABOUT THOSE COLORED PENCILS . . .

42

THE WIND REALLY PICKED UP!!

AND THE ROAD'S SO SLICK, I HAVE TO BE CAREFUL WE DON'T --

Squeak Squeak

HYDROPLANE!!!

AHHHHH!!

SLIIIIIIIIIIIIIIIIDE~

≥GASP≤ I CAN BARELY SEE FIVE FEET AHEAD!

WE'RE GOING TO PULL OVER AND WAIT THIS STORM OUT.

DO WE REALLY HAVE TO PITCH A TENT IN THIS RAIN, MOM?

WELL... I SUPPOSE WE COULD SPRING FOR A CABIN.... JUST THIS ONCE.

47

THE NEXT MORNING

OOF.

IS IT STILL RAINING?

I DON'T THINK SO. . . .

Peek!

EW, LOOK.

POOR FROG!

Shudder

NOTHING LIKE A BUNCH OF DEAD ANIMALS TO START YOUR MORNING OFF RIGHT.

AND SO:

I'M CALLING MINE BUBBLY.

I'M CALLING MINE ROSEMARIE.

FISH FOOD

YOUR FISH POOED!

53

...A CHAMELEON??

COOOOOOL!!

DON'T WORRY! MY BUDDY FRANK BREEDS 'EM. HE SAYS THEY'RE PRETTY INDESTRUCTIBLE.

AT THE PET STORE

THEY EAT CRICKETS??

UH-HUH, AND WE'RE HAVING A SALE! FIVE DOLLARS FOR TWENTY!

THIS SEEMS LIKE A LOT OF CRICKETS, DAD. . . .

chirp chirp chirp chirp chirp chir chirp chirp chirp chirp chirp ch chirp chir chirp chirp chirp chirp ch chirp chir

YEP! LELAND'S GONNA BE IN FOODIE PARADISE!

chirp chirp chirp chirp chirp chirp chirp Ch chir chi

56

HE STILL HASN'T EATEN ANY.

MAYBE HE'S A LITTLE INTIMIDATED.

BUT I'LL BET THAT, BY MORNING, HE'LL HAVE EATEN A FEW.

chirp chirp chirp
chirp chirp chirp
chirp chirp chi
Chirp

OKAY, GIRLS. **NO MORE PETS** FOR A WHILE.

NO FAIR. YOU NEVER GET US ANY **GOOD** PETS ANYWAY.

MAYBE ANOTHER TIME, A. FOR NOW, WE NEED THE EXTRA SPACE!

WHAT FOR?

WELL . . . YOU'RE GOING TO BE GETTING A LITTLE BROTHER!

pat pat

. . .

READY TO SEE SOME DINOSAURS, WILL?

YEAH!!

DINOSAURS. DIEEEE-NO-SAUR. DINOOOOOO. DI-DI-DI-DI-DI...

Tappity Tappity

Whap Whap

Tap Tap

CAN'T YOU BE EXCITED **QUIETLY?!!!**

Dinosaur National Monument
Visitor Center/Dinosaur Quarry
5 MILES AHEAD

DIEEEE-NO-SAUR...

OH MAN, WHY IS UTAH A MILLION DEGREES?

I THOUGHT YOU LOVED HOT WEATHER.

YEAH, BUT I'M NOT **USED** TO IT! SAN FRANCISCO IS FREEZING IN SUMMER.

DINOSAUR
NATIONAL MONUMENT
FOSSIL BONE QUARRY

IF WE WERE SWIMMING, THIS WOULD BE FINE.

DON'T EVEN THINK ABOUT IT.

AWWWH! CAN I GET THIS TRUCK, MOM??

I SUPPOSE EACH OF YOU CAN CHOOSE **ONE** SOUVENIR.

scratch scratch scratch

Dino Dig Vehicle

?

Tap Tap

OOH! OOH! BACK SCRATCHER!! YES!

WELL, KIDS . . .

WELCOME to COLORFUL COLORADO

ONE MORE NIGHT OF CAMPING, AND TOMORROW WE'LL SEE YOUR COUSINS!

VRRRRRRRM!

LET'S SEE . . .

COLORADO: THE CENTENNIAL STATE.

THAT'S NO FUN.

SCR EEE EEE EEE!

I WAS HOPING IT WOULD BE, LIKE, "BEARS EAT YOUR LITTLE BROTHER STATE."

YEAH. . . .

NEEEERRR-OWWWWWWW! GSSSHHH! VROOOOOM!!!

YOUR MOM AND I LIKE THE NAME WILL.

WILLY! HI, WILLY!

NOT WILLY. JUST WILL.

AH!

WILLY WAS YOUR GRANDMA'S DOG'S NAME. . . .

?

WHEREAS YOUR BROTHER IS HERE BECAUSE OF THE **WILL OF GOD**.

URRK.

66

67

WAAAH! WAAAH! WAH!

GROOOAN.

I CAN'T SLEEEEP! WHY DOESN'T MOM MAKE THAT BABY BE QUIET?

≥HIC≤ ≥COUGH≤ WAAAAAAHHHH . . .

IF MOM HAD THAT SUPERPOWER, I THINK SHE'D USE IT ON YOU, TOO. . . .

AHWAAAAA AAAAHHHH . . .

crunch crunch

SLRRRP

crunch crunch

DENIS, YOU'LL TAKE RAINA TO THE BUS STOP ON YOUR WAY TO WORK?

UH-HUH. READY, RAINA?

ALMOST.

AND I'LL TAKE AMARA TO PRE-SCH --

SWAT

I'M NOT GOING.

IT'S NOT EASY HAVING SO MANY OF US IN ONE HOUSE, HUH?

I DUNNO.

YOUR MOM ASKED ME TO DO SOMETHING WITH YOU AND YOUR SISTER THIS WEEKEND. HOW 'BOUT WE GO TO THE ZOO?

OKAY.

AND SO:

C'MON, A! IT'S DADDY-DAUGHTER DAY.

MMM.

I'M TAKING YOU AND RAINA OUT. JUST THE THREE OF US!

MNH.

WE'RE GOING TO THE ZOO. . . .

72

BUT WHAT'S WRONG WITH SNAKES?

I HATE THEM.

BUT THEY'RE SO COOL!

THEY'RE DISGUSTING.

REPTILE

BUT WH --

FINE!

I'LL TELL YOU WHY. BEFORE YOU WERE BORN . . .

. . . WE WENT CAMPING. I WAS OBSESSED WITH PICKING BLACKBERRIES.

75

82

83

THIS IS AMAZING! THIS IS INCREDIBLE! I WISH I COULD TAKE A PICTURE!!

YOUR DAD AND I USED TO DO THIS ALL THE TIME WHEN WE WERE YOUNGER.

I WISH DADDY WAS HERE RIGHT NOW.

I WISH DAD WAS HERE, TOO.

DAD WOULD'VE GOTTEN US McDONALD'S.

...BUT I DON'T **WANT** TACOS!

TOO BAD!

I! WANT! Mc! DONALD'S!

YOU CAN'T **HAVE** MCDONALD'S!

I COULD GO AND GET YOU SOME McDONALD'S....

DENIS!

SHE'S NEVER GOING TO LEARN!

SHE'S NEVER GOING TO STOP SCREAMING!

NO. BOTH OF YOU, **NO.** AMARA, GO TO YOUR ROOM.

HISSSS...

A dream where Dad still has a job...

A dream where we didn't just
get a new baby brother...

A dream where I never even
got the sister I asked for.

A dream where someone is going to put their arms around me and tell me...

IT'S GOING TO BE OKAY.

LATER

BLAH BLAH JOB SEARCH...
BLAH BLAH WANT ADS...
BLAH BLAH ECONOMY...

MAYBE IT'S TIME I THOUGHT ABOUT FINISHING COLLEGE.

MAYBE.

EW, WHY WOULD ANYONE **WANT** TO GO TO SCHOOL?

TO GET A GOOD JOB.

HOW ARE YOUR LETTERS TO SANTA COMING, GIRLS?

GOOD! I ASKED FOR WORLD PEACE, SOME NEW MARKERS, A JOB FOR DAD, AND THE NEWEST BABY-SITTERS CLUB BOOK!

WHAT ABOUT YOU, AMARA?

a SnAke

ICK! BLECH! GROSS!

YOU MIGHT WANT TO ASK FOR SOMETHING ELSE, HONEY. . . .

MERRY ⪦SNIFF⪧ CHRISTMAS!

WE'VE LEVELED OFF, AMARA.
YOU SHOULD FEEL BETTER SOON!

AAAAUGH...
AAAAUGH...

RAINA, I HAVE TO SWITCH
HIGHWAYS -- CAN YOU
NAVIGATE?

UH...

THIS IS CONFUSING...
I THINK YOU WANT TO
TAKE I-70 E. . . .

I'M ALREADY
ON I-70 E.

OH, OKAY. TAKE
EXIT 470 TO CO-260 -- NO,
SORRY, EXIT 260 TO CO-470.

EXIT
270?

NO, 260!

WE JUST MISSED
260!!

ARE THESE ALL NEW HOUSES, MOM?

UH-HUH. I THINK THIS HOUSING DEVELOPMENT IS ABOUT THREE YEARS OLD.

2753 POPLAR COURT... THIS IS THE PLACE.

SO, PENELOPE, WHAT'S YOUR THING?

MY . . . THING?

YEAH. DO YOU LIKE RAP MUSIC? HORROR MOVIES? *BEVERLY HILLS, 90210?*

OH. I LIKE COMICS!

YEAH?? LIKE BATMAN? HULK? X-MEN?

I LIKE CALVIN AND HOBBES, FOR BETTER OR FOR WORSE, FOXTROT . . .

PSSH. THOSE AREN'T **REAL** COMICS.

SLAM

DAD!

WHEN DID **YOU** GET HERE??

YOUR UNCLE JIM JUST PICKED ME UP AT THE AIRPORT!

SLLLP

DO AMARA AND WILL KNOW YOU'RE HERE?

THEY'RE BOTH ASLEEP. YOU MUST BE PRETTY TIRED, TOO!

YAWWWN . . . YEAH, MAYBE I'LL GO GET READY FOR --

KARAOKE PARTY!!!

WHO'S IN??

MAYBE I'LL GO GET READY FOR A KARAOKE PARTY??

WOOO!

EVERYONE! I HAVE WONDERFUL NEWS!

I GOT A NEW JOB!!

OH, THANK GOODNESS!

THIS CALLS FOR A CELEBRATION! I'M TAKING YOU ALL OUT FOR A NICE DINNER.

McDONALD'S??!

NO, BURGER KING!!

AMARA, YOUR DINNER'S GETTING COLD.

click
click

AMARA, IT'S PAST YOUR BEDTIME.

click click
click
click click
click

AMARA, BAMBI'S ON TV.

MADE YA LOOK.

GRRRRRR!!!

Click click
Click
Click
Click
Click

Hee hee   Giggle

Ha Ha! *Snort*

PENELOPE STILL SLEEPS WITH A TEDDY BEAR!!

HUH?? WHAT ARE YOU GUYS DOING IN HERE?

Ha Ha   Ha Ha

UH, THIS IS MY DEN? WE'RE EATING BREAKFAST.

WHAT ARE YOU -- THIRTEEN?

I'M FOURTEEN.

HAAAAAAA HA HA HA HA HA HA!!

LINDSAY SURE HAS A LOT OF BEAUTY PRODUCTS....

EW, WHAT DID YOU DO TO YOUR FACE?!

OKAY IF I SIT WITH YOU GUYS?

SO, LINDSAY! ARE YOU STILL INTO SKATING?

HUH?

ANYWAY. JEREMY, HAVE YOU SEEN THE NEW GUNS N' ROSES VIDEO?

YES.

BLAH BLAH HEAVY METAL . . . BLAH BLAH LEATHER FASHIONS . . . BLAH BLAH BIG HAIR . . .

Ha ha.

HAAAAAHAHAHAHA!! GNARLY! HIGH FIVE!!

Ha Ha Ha Ha Ha

SORRY, PENELOPE -- WE'RE HALFWAY THROUGH THIS GAME. WE'LL DEAL YOU IN NEXT TIME, OKAY?

134

HEY, LISTEN . . .

I . . . I **DID** BRING COLORED PENCILS ON THIS TRIP. I HID THEM IN MY SUITCASE.

YOU WANT TO USE THEM? I'LL TOTALLY GO GET THEM FOR YOU.

NAH.

LIKE I SAID . . . I DON'T REALLY CARE.

SIGH . . . THE COUSIN I WISHED WAS MY SISTER BARELY KNOWS ME AT ALL.

AND THE SISTER I ACTUALLY HAVE HATES ME.

ALTHOUGH I GUESS IT'S NOTHING PERSONAL . . .

SHE HATES EVERYONE.

KIDS, YOUR MOM AND I HAVE MADE AN EXECUTIVE DECISION.

I KNOW WE'VE ALL BEEN CRAMPED AND CROWDED IN THIS LITTLE APARTMENT FOR YEARS....

AND YOU GUYS WOULD ALL LIKE A BIT OF EXTRA PRIVACY, SO --

WE'RE MOVING?!

WE'VE DECIDED TO GIVE RAINA HER OWN BEDROOM.

OH.

... OH. **OH!!!**

NO FAIR!!

BUT I STILL HAFTA SHARE A ROOM WITH WILL?!

RAINA'S GROWING UP, HONEY. SHE NEEDS SOME SPACE.

WAIT, WE ONLY HAVE TWO BEDROOMS. . . . WHERE ARE YOU AND DAD GONNA SLEEP?

WE'LL MOVE INTO THE LIVING ROOM.

WOW, YOU'D DO THAT FOR ME?

YOU'D DO THAT FOR HER?!

WE KNEW YOU'D FEEL A LITTLE PUT OUT BECAUSE OF ALL THIS, AMARA . . .

SO, WE'RE GOING TO BUY YOU THAT SNAKE YOU'VE BEEN WANTING.

WHAT?!

Peek!

AAAAAAUGH! HE'S CRAWLING OUT!!!

HE'S, HE'S . . .

HE'S CLIMBING UP INTO THE CAR SEAT!!

GRAB HIM!!

NO WAY! HE'LL **BITE** ME!!

WE HAVE TO DO SOMETHING!

THERE'S A SNAKE IN THE VAN?!?!

BUT AREN'T YOU GLAD WE TOLD YOU **AFTER** PICKING YOU UP FROM GIRL SCOUTS?

AAAAAAA

Sssssssss...

Sssssssss...

Sssssssssss...

SNAKE?!!

IT'S JUST UNCLE BILL FRYING BACON, YOU MORON.

SSS SSSS

154

YOU ALWAYS HAVE TO STEAL MY THUNDER!!

WHATEVER -- YOU HAVEN'T DRAWN ALL WEEK!

SO?!

GIRLS, YOU ARE **BOTH** ARTISTS! ALWAYS HAVE BEEN, ALWAYS WILL BE. YOU HAVE THAT IN **COMMON**.

WHY CAN'T YOU TWO GET ALONG?

YOU JUST SPENT A WEEK ARGUING WITH **YOUR** BROTHERS AND SISTERS.

LET'S GO.

HOW IS THAT DIFFERENT?

YEAH!

NO, REALLY, MOM, EXPLAIN!

YEAH, WE'RE LISTENING!

SIGH

156

DENIS, YOU **KNOW** WE HAVE EVERYTHING WE NEED.

I JUST --

YOU WORRY TOO MUCH! WE'LL BE FINE.

FLIGHT 56 IS NOW BOARDING FOR SAN FRANCISCO. . . .

NOW GO HOME AND WATCH BASEBALL ALL WEEK, AND GRIND YOUR COFFEE AS EARLY IN THE MORNING AS YOU PLEASE.

#56 San Francisco
12:40p

. . .

. . .

NOW YOU KNOW THE **REAL** REASON I CAN'T RIDE HOME WITH YOU, WILL.

ANOTHER WEEK IN THE CAR. **FUN.**

IT'LL BE INTERESTING, RAINA....

WE'RE GOING TO DRIVE HOME ALONG THE **SOUTHERN** ROUTE!

SO IT'LL BE EVEN HOTTER?

KNOCK
KNOCK

DID YOU GET THE SNAKE OUT OF THE CAR?

NOT YET.

THEN I'M NOT COMING OUT.

YOU CAN'T STAY IN YOUR ROOM FOREVER!

She lured me out with cookies

OKAY. LET ME GET THIS STRAIGHT....

MANGO IS A KING SNAKE, AND KING SNAKES ONLY EAT **LIVE** MICE....

UH-HUH.

HEY, MOM?

UH-HUH?

I JUST REALIZED YOU NEVER KISSED DAD GOOD-BYE. HOW COME?

. . .

AND WHEN HE SAID HE'D DRIVE YOU CRAZY...

...THAT WAS JUST A JOKE, RIGHT?

RAINA, DON'T BE AN IDIOT.

HEY! I'M NOT AN IDIOT! I'M JUST ASKING A QUESTION!

AN **IDIOTIC** QUESTION!

THAT'S OKAY....

YOUR DAD AND I... WELL, WE...

WE WANTED TO SPEND SOME TIME APART THIS SUMMER.

I THOUGHT HE COULDN'T DRIVE WITH US BECAUSE OF **WORK!**

THAT'S PART OF THE REASON, TOO.

170

JUST SOME DUDE IN A TRUCK.

THEY'RE GETTING IN! THEY'RE WAVING! BYE, MOM! DON'T GET KILLED!

OF **COURSE** WILL THINKS THIS IS THE COOLEST DAY OF HIS LIFE.

AND SO:

179

CHILL OUT, WOULD YOU?

CHILL OUT? **CHILL OUT?!**

WE'RE IN THE MIDDLE OF NOWHERE... IT'S A MILLION DEGREES...

MOM AND WILL ARE OUT THERE WITH GOD KNOWS WHO, AND NOW...

BEEEEEEEEEEOOP.

!

AND NOW MY STUPID WALKMAN'S DEAD AGAIN!!

FLING!

AND SO:

SCReeeeeeee

EAT **NOM** GRUB **YUM**
SNARF SHOVEL

GIRLS, I AM **SO SORRY.**

I DON'T KNOW WHAT I WAS THINKING!

LEAVING YOU TWO ALL ALONE . . . WHAT IF SOMETHING HAD HAPPENED TO YOU?

IT'S OKAY, MOM.

FINDING A RIDE FOR FOUR WOULD'VE BEEN HARDER THAN TWO.

AND ANYWAY, WE SURVIVED! RIGHT, RAINA?

BARELY.

193

Photo Album

After I wrote the script for this book, my dad sent me this photo, which I had forgotten about. This picture pretty much encapsulates *Sisters* in a nutshell. We're about six and one here.

My mom took this picture of Amara and me sitting on top of a hamper in our upstairs hallway. The photo still hangs in the same spot.

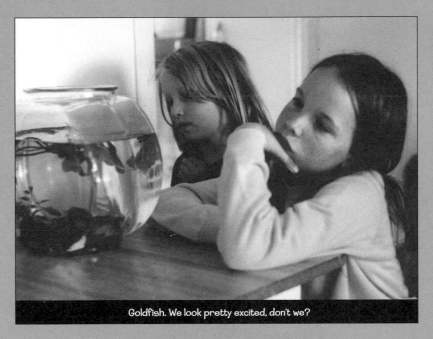

Goldfish. We look pretty excited, don't we?

Here we are around the time this book takes place: ages fourteen, nine, and six. Amara had just won first place in an art contest I'd gotten an honorable mention for, a few years prior. I'm hiding my jealousy well!

Thanks to...

My family, obviously: my mom, dad, brother, sister, aunts, uncles, cousins, and grandparents. Thank you for letting me mine our collective history (and photo albums) for story ideas!

My husband, Dave Roman, who is invaluable in every way.

My editors David Saylor and Cassandra Pelham, and the tireless team at Scholastic: Sheila Marie Everett, Lizette Serrano, Candace Greene, Phil Falco, Bess Braswell, Whitney Steller, Tracy van Straaten, Ed Masessa, David Levithan, Lori Benton, Ellie Berger, John Mason, Antonio Gonzalez, Emily Heddleson, Starr Baer, Jaime Capifali, and all the wonderful folks whose time and space dovetail with mine.

My agent, Judy Hansen, for working her magic.

Braden Lamb for his stellar coloring, as well as Shelli Paroline and Chris O'Neil for color assistance.

John Green, for tech wizardry and his nifty lettering.

Jerzy and Anne Drozd, my beta readers.

My wonderful fans, who keep me smiling, and make it all worthwhile.

—Raina

Raina Telgemeier grew up in San Francisco, then moved to New York City, where she earned an illustration degree at the School of Visual Arts. She is the creator of *Smile*, a #1 *New York Times* bestselling graphic memoir based on her childhood. It won a Will Eisner Award for Best Publication for Teens, received a Boston Globe-Horn Book Honor, and has appeared on many state reading lists. She is also the creator of *Drama*, a #1 *New York Times* bestseller and the recipient of a Stonewall Book Award Honor. It was selected as an ALSC Notable Children's Book and one of YALSA's Top Ten Great Graphic Novels for Teens. Raina also adapted and illustrated The Baby-sitters Club graphic novels, which were selected for YALSA's Great Graphic Novels for Teens list and *Booklist*'s Top 10 Graphic Novels for Youth list.

Raina lives in Astoria, New York, with her husband and fellow cartoonist, Dave Roman. To learn more about Raina, visit her online at www.goRaina.com.

Also by
Raina Telgemeier

This is the true story of how Raina severely injured her two front teeth when she was in the sixth grade, and the dental drama – on top of boy confusion, a major earthquake, and friends who turn out to be not so friendly – that followed!

Callie is the set designer for her middle school's spring musical, and is determined to create a set worthy of Broadway. But between the onstage AND offstage drama that occurs once the actors are chosen, it's going to be a long way until opening night!